1 MONTH OF
FREE
READING

at

www.ForgottenBooks.com

By purchasing this book you are eligible for one month membership to ForgottenBooks.com, giving you unlimited access to our entire collection of over 1,000,000 titles via our web site and mobile apps.

To claim your free month visit:

www.forgottenbooks.com/free145832

ISBN 978-0-483-70669-9
PIBN 10145832

AM I A GOOD TEACHER?

WILLIAM M. WEMETT

Am I A Good Teacher?

BY

William M. Wemett, A. M., Ped. B.

Supervisor of Training School and Professor
of Methods, State Normal School,
Valley City, N. D.

"Oh wad some power the giftie gie us

To see oursel's as others see us!

It wad frae monie a blunder free us."

—Burns.

PUBLISHED BY

THE CAPITAL SUPPLY COMPANY

EDUCATIONAL PUBLISHERS

Pierre, S. D.

COPYRIGHT 1915, CAPITAL SUPPLY COMPANY

Table of Contents

PREFACE.

This little book is meant for the thousands of young people who enter the teaching profession every year. Its purpose is two fold: to give, in brief form, the untrained beginner an intelligent standard by which to judge of his own teaching ability, and to furnish both the trained and the untrained teacher a constant reminder of the myriads of little things which vitally affect a teacher's success.

The contents of the book are based upon the familiar fact that more teachers fail through their conduct outside of school than through a lack of teaching ability—hence the large proportion of space given to matters of character, conduct and appearance. The question form is used because it is more personal, and therefore, more effective. These pages are not meant to be read with pleasure, but to be thought through with profit.

The writer wishes to express his thanks to Dr. and Mrs. Charles A. McMurry, of De Kalb, Ill., for their careful reading and criticism of the subject matter. He is indebted also to Miss Minnie J. Neilson, County Superintendent of Barnes county, North Dakota, and to Prof. M. C. James, Dr. Willis G. Bell and Miss Mary Gardner of the faculty of the State Normal School at Valley City for their helpful snggestions upon the purpose and plan of the book.

W. M. WEMETT,
Valley City, March 5, 1915.

MY CHARACTER.

1. Do I habitually do things which I would not want my parents to do, or to know of my doing?

2. When an attractive opportunity to do wrong arises, do I have to think it over and decide, or do I instinctively and almost automatically do what is right?

3. Is my life, both public and private, a good example for my pupils?

4. Am I more concerned about what I do, or about what my friends know of my doing?

5. Do I rise above the drudgery and irritating incidents of my work?

6. Do I know myself? Do I take advantage of my strong points and guard myself against my weaknesses?

7. Am I fearless or merely foolhardy?

8. Am I controlled more by the forces within me, or by the forces without?

9. Do I adhere to the right and spurn the wrong without regard to the person involved?

10. Am I willing to be true at the expense of popularity?

11. In the last analysis, am I guided by principles or by policy?

MY PERSONALTY.

1. Have I a personality of my own or am I a reflection?

2. Do I feel at home among people of culture and position?

3. Do I make myself equally at home among people of humble occupation and limited education?

4. Do I carry the stamp of a cultured home, so that a stranger would recognize it after five minutes conversation?

5. Am I a leader or a campfollower?

6. Do people enjoy meeting me and having me with them?

7. Have I a hearty but refined sense of humor?

8. Do I wear my heart upon my sleeve, or do I hold my deeper thoughts and feelings in reserve?

.9. Do I always have something worth while to contribute to the life of the people I meet?

10. Can I dominate a situation without domineering over the people present?

11. Do I know how to be frivolous upon occasions?

12. Could it ever be said that I have "a fatty enlargement of the ego"?

13. Am I well balanced, or is my enthusiasm for some things apt to run away with my judgment?

MY DISPOSITION.

1. Am I happy? Do I show it? Do I make others so?

2. Am I really interested in other people, or do my thoughts, feelings and wants revolve about myself?

3. Am I open and frank with people, enough so that they are really acquainted with me and I with them?

4. Have I the habit of saying pleasant things, and do I enjoy it?

5. When there is some volunteer work to be done do I step forward quickly and do my share or do I wait in hope that someone else will do it?

6. Does my mind dwell more upon my rights or upon my opportunities?

7. Am I pessimistic or hopeful? Do I look at the doughnut or at the hole?

8. Can I look into a mud-puddle and see anything except the mud?

9. Do I like to gossip?

10. When I fail, do I complain of poor tools, and, when I succeed, take the credit to myself?

11. Am I given to moods of depression and hilarity, or am I blessed with an even disposition?

MY PERSONAL APPEARANCE.

1. Do I walk with confidence, energy and dignity?

2. Do I often stand on one foot and lean against something when talking?

3. Is my spinal column bone or gelatine?

4. Are my shoes and hair well groomed?

5. Are my teeth and finger nails clean?

6. Is my linen clean? Are my clothes well pressed?

7. Do I chew gum, giggle and use perfume freely?

8. Do my clothes display the latest styles, or reflect the best taste?

9. Do my clothes tone down my peculiarities of person or exaggerate them?

10. Which would a stranger notice first, me or my clothes?

MY HEALTH.

1. Have I any physical deformities which render my constant appearance before small children undesirable for the children?

2. Have I vitality enough to do my work with ease and to spare, or am I tired out by my day's work?

3. Have I a full allowance of human energy and vitality? If not, why not?

4. Am I out of school frequently? Do

I cut corners in my work because of poor health or lack of strength?

5. Am I so nervous as to be easily irritated by the children?

6. Have I any contageous or infectious diseases such as tuberculosis or eczema which makes my presence dangerous to the children?

7. Have I any chronic difficulties such as epilepsy, hysteria or frequent fainting spells which are likely to cause disturbing accidents in the school room?

MY PROFESSIONAL SPIRIT.

1. What is my motive in being a teacher?

2. Do my characteristics fit me for teaching, or for some other walk of life?

3. Is teaching my profession, or my occupation?

4. Have I taken up teaching permanently, or just while I am waiting?

5. Do I attend and take part in educational associations and teacher's institutes, or try to dodge them?

6. Do I seize every opportunity to become acquainted with the leading educators of the state, their institutions and their work?

7. Am I familiar with the educational system and school laws of the state?

8. Do I really like to work or do I look forward to Friday nights and holidays?

9. Do I figure out how I can get more salary or how I can be more valuable to the school?

10. Do I take one or more professional magazines?

11. Do I keep posted on current educational problems and methods?

12. Do I possess a small professional library? Do I use it and add to it from time to time?

13. In my professional reading, do I distinguish between sound pedagogy and professional twaddle?

14. Do I study the needs of my school carefully?

15. Do I know my work as an engineer knows his engine?

16. Am I so wrapped up in my line of work that I cannot recognize the equal value of my neighbors?

17. Do I look upon teaching as a life sentence, or as a life of service?

MY SCHOLARSHIP.

1. Do I keep just ahead of the class in my knowledge of the subject, or have I a broad and deep fund of information to draw from?

2. Do I know enough about the subjects I am teaching so I can produce good illustrations on a moment's notice?

3. Do I know my subject well enough to see the relation between today's lesson and the whole subject, and the relation between this subject and other subjects?

4. Do I keep broadening my knowledge of the subject by continued study?

5. Do I keep studying more and more into the physical and mental nature of children?

6. Do I ever have to lean upon the textbook during a recitation or ask the class to look up for to-morrow something I do not know to-day?

7. Is my scholarship manifest in my conversation, my letters and my manners?

8. Is my scholarship large enough so people can notice it without my flirting it in their faces?

9. Is my scholarship worthy of my pupils' admiration? Should it be?

10. Is there a large gap between what I know and what I think I know?

11. Do I know any one subject with un-usual thoroughness?

12. How much of my knowledge is first hand, from the sources?

13. Does what I know burden me, and others?

14. What percentage of my knowledge can I use?

15. Is my information up-to-date or rather threadbare?

16. Does what I know ever stand in the way of my knowing more?

17. Is my knowledge of things definite enough so I can put my finger upon figures, names and places, or is it somewhat uncertain and vague?

MY KNOWLEDGE OF CHILDREN.

1. Do I understand my pupils as well as I do the subject I am teaching them? Does good teaching require this?

2. Do I constantly and carefully study the nature, disposition, habits, likes and dis-likes of my pupils?

3. Can I intelligently judge of the educa-tional value of material, books, pictures, songs, etc., without an intelligent knowledge of child nature?

4. Can I intelligently adjust my teach-ing to each child?

5. Do I take advantage of the pride, am-bition, curiosity, pugnacity, sense of duty, sense of ownership, likes and dislikes of each child to make him enjoy his work and do his best?

6. Do I try to treat all children alike when I know they are different?

7. Do I consider the peculiarities of each child in disciplining him.

8. Do I know how my pupils live, how they are fed, what they do outside of school,

and know how these things affect their school work?

9. Do I take advantage of the child's peculiarities of disposition in, correcting his habits and in improving his character?

10. Do I realize the extreme importance to the child of good food, good rest and fresh air, and the duty of the teacher in these matters?

11. Do I take advantage of the compelling force of imitation in small children, and keep before them the good, the beautiful, the noble, and keep from them all that is unworthy of imitation?

12 Should a child's activity be repressed or directed?

13. Do I ever talk to parents about the importance of the period of adolescence in the normal development of their child?

✓ 14. Do I realize that love is the greatest factor in the education of a child? Which of my pupils need it most?

MY PROFESSIONAL TRAINING.

1. Have I had a normal school training or a similar opportunity to have my teaching ability examined and criticised by those who know good teaching?

2. Do I make a study of the science of teaching and keep up-to-date in it, or do I follow those who believe that such a science either does not exist or is unnecessary?

3. Am I getting my professional training at the expense of the children rather than spend the time and money attending a professional school?

4. How much of the following items have been well provided for in my professional training? (1) Psychology and Child Study. (2) Methods of Teaching. (3) School Management. (4) History and Philosophy of Educa-

tion.   (5) Practice teaching under competent supervision.   Am I well trained for teaching without a mastery of all of these subjects?

5.   Will a college education, mature years, good common sense and enthusiasm fit a person for teaching without professional study and training?

6.   How many books on teaching are there in my library?   How many of them have I studied?   How far do they influence my teaching.

7.   Have I a correct standard of what good teaching is?   How do I know that it is correct?

8.   Where did I get my standard of teaching, from good teachers, from the best professioual books, or from a school board which itself had no correct standard, and from my imagination?

9.   Is experience sufficient training for a teacher?   Is it possible that untrained experience might prevent one from ever becoming a good teacher?

MY RESPONSIBILITY.

I.   Do I realize that all other good qualities cannot make a good teacher, if responsibility is lacking?

2.   Am I man enough, or woman enough, to carry a great trust?

3.   Am I usually to be relied upon, or always?

4.   Is my word as good as the deed, and accepted as such by those who know me?

5.   Do I feel an impelling moral obligation to meet appointments, no matter how trivial or with whom they are made, meet them on time, and offer no excuses?

6.   Have I read Elbert Hubbard's "A Message to Garcia"?   Am I a Roman?

7. Do I realize that responsibility is the outgrowth of long and persistent effort, and is not to drop down upon me all at once?

8. Do I develop responsibility in the children by giving them responsibility and throwing them upon their own resources, or merely by telling them that they must develop it?

MY HABITS OF EFFICIENCY.

1. Do I start things which I never finish?
2. Am I always on time?
3. Do I keep appointments promptly?
4. Do I meet every occasion prepared?
5. Do I waste time?
6. Do I putter?
7. Do I neglect things?
8. Do I fret and worry?
9. Do I try to do too much?
10. Do I try to do more than one thing at a time?
11. Do I systematize my work?
12. Have I a place for everything?
13. Do I organize my time?
14. Do I prevent others from wasting my time?
15. Do I alphabetize things?
16. Do I make use of odd moments?
17. Do I work quickly without hurrying?
18. How many times do I have to be told to do a thing?
19. Do spurts ever make experts? Do I work by jerks and spasms?
20. Can I give attention to details without being fussy?
21 Have I the "prompt" habit, the "sure" habit, the "system" habit, the "organization" habit, the "careful" habit and the "think" habit?

MY BUSINESS ABILITY.

1. Do I make my word good at any cost?

2. Do I begin every business transaction with a full and frank understanding of just what my responsibilities and duties are?

3. Before I accept a teaching position, do I know whether I am expected to do the janitor work?

4. Do I ever attempt to change positions without being honorably released?

5. Do I pay my bills regularly?

6. In handling money for some society or organization, do I keep careful account of their funds, and keep them entirely separate from my own?

7. Do I either pay by checks or take a receipt?

8. Do I keep an account book, and keep it carefully?

9. Am I economical?

10. Can I be economical without being "tight"?

11. Do I weigh business matters carefully, consult with good business men, and proceed conservatively?

MY PATIENCE.

1. Is it necessary to be impatient in order to make progress?

2. Have I the sympathy with children which should guide my patience?

3. Am I as patient with the children in my charge as I would expect a teacher to be with my own child?

4. Do I sometimes compare the plodding child's ability with my own, instead of comparing it with what mine was at his age?

5. Do I make a sharp distinction between being patient and being "easy"?

6. Is it necessary to be slow in order to be patient?

7. Do I know when patience ceases to be a virtue?

8. Is my patience so prominent that it destroys my decision and leadership?

9. Is it possible that what I call my patience is only a lack of push?

MY GROWTH.

1. Am I more interested in teaching, and enjoying it more, than when I began?

2. Am I more professional than when I began teaching?

3. Do I find a monotonous routine about my work? If so, will not a study and application of new methods bring back the pleasure and enthusiasm of teaching?

4. Do I feel that my salary is not being increased as it should be? Am I actually more valuable to the school than I was last year? In what ways?

5. How much time out of school do I spend improving myself?

6. Am I pursuing any systematic course of study to improve my teaching?

7. Am I taking a more useful part in the life of the community than I did last year.

8. Have I a broader acquaintance and more friends than I had last year?

9. What improvements have I accomplished in my school recently?

10. Am I becoming more liberal in my views and more sympathetic in spirit?

MY TACT.

1. On approaching a person on business, do I express my opinion first, or ask for his?

2. In broaching a proposition to a person, do I first look at it from his point of view?

3. Am I in the habit of noticing the good qualities in my associates and of mentioning

them occassionally, or is it a matter of criticism about which I usually speak to them?

4. Do I tell those under my direction what to do, or lead them to my wishes by asking their opinions?

5. Do I say "Please", "Thank you," and "Good morning" frequently and cordially?

6. Do I smile with my heart, or with my lips?

7. Do the nice things I say smack more of flattery or of sincerity?

8. Do I merely say nice things, or do them?

9. Do my words and my actions say the same thing?

10. Am I independent, or merely blunt?

11. Is a pound of cleverness worth as much as an ounce of loyalty?

12. Would more frankness, sincerity and loyalty make me more tactful?

13. Am I as respectful to other people as I expect them to be to me?

MY ENGLISH.

1. Can I read ordinary English in a forceful attractive manner, or is expression largely lost in poor pronunciation, indistinct enunciation and lack of emphasis?

2. Is slang prominent in my conversation?

3. Am I a complete master of the usual errors of grammar, such as "done", "seem", "haint", "that there", "such like", "set", "haint got", etc?

4. Can I express myself clearly and forcefully before an audience?

5. Can I write a paper to be published or read at an educational association, and make it interesting, original and free from threadbare platitudes?

6. Can I adapt my English to the understanding of small children?

7. In speaking, do I hesitate, "hem" and have to grope for words?

8. Is it probable that my associates ever speak of my English as being exceptionally good or exceptionally poor?

9. Am I in the habit of reading a great deal of good English?

·10· Before I speak or write a sentence, do I form in my mind exactly what I want to say?

11. Do I try to use good English only when speaking to cultured people, or all the time?

. 12. Do I ever allow a mistake in spelling to pass through my hands?

13. In speaking, do I separate my words distinctly, or run them all in together?

14. Do I open my mouth in speaking, or mumble through my teeth and lips?

15. Do I speak with expression and emphasis, or drag along in a monotone?

16. Do I speak directly to the point, or beat around the bush?

17. Do I stop speaking when I have finished what I started out to say?

MY CONVERSATION.

1. Which is the more important thing in my conversation, my ideas, or my words and manner?

2. Are the ideas I express my own, or the reflection of the opinion which is held by the person to whom I am speaking?

3. Is my conversation fresh and original, or is it hemmed in by conventionalities and platitudes?

4. Do I make myself prominent in my conversation, or is my friend and his interest the chief topic?

5. Had I rather hear myself talk, or listen to my friend?

6.   In an argumentative conversation, do I ever win my argument and loose my friend's respect?

7.   Do I manifest a genuine personal interest in my friend, or is my conversation such that it might be directed to any one of a number of people?

8.   Do I meet new acquaintances half way, or do I expect them to do most of the getting acquainted?

9.   Have I formed the habit of enjoying to meet new people?

10.   Do I ever try to "make an impression"?

11.   Do I gush?

12.   Do I look my friend in the eye, .or gaze around the room while speaking to him?

MY CORRESPONDENCE.

1.   Do I answer letters as promptly as I desire others to answer mine?

2.   Am I willing to have my character and efficiency judged from my letter?

3.   Do I take advantage of the opportunity which correspondence offers for making and retaining friends?

4.   Do I use society stationery in business letters?

5.   Do I always use correct grammar and correct spelling?

6.   Is there a tone of respect in my letters?

MY POLITICS.

1.   Can I be an active citizen without getting into politics?

2.   In my mind, are principles greater than policies and men larger than parties?

3.   Should I do what is right, or what is consistent?

4.   I grant freedom of thought and of speech to those who agree with me. What about the others?

5. Did I inherit my political belief, or acquire it by study of men and conditions?

6. Do I believe in the cure of public evils, or in their prevention?

7. Do I read the papers which are on my side, on the other side, or on neither side? Do I read any paper?

8. Is there a right place and a wrong place for me to discuss political questions?

9. Can I throw mud without getting my hands dirty?

10. Should I stay out of a bad situation, or get into it and improve it?

11. Can I talk intelligently about the local, state and national political situation?

MY RELIGION.

1. Do I do a man's work, or a woman's work, in some church organization?

2. Is my religion of such a nature that I feel a clash between it and my school duties?

3. Do I bring up questions of creed and belief in my class discussions?

4. Do I make my religious ideas known by talking them, or by living them?

5. Am I willing to deprive myself of some pleasures, which I believe are entirely right, in order to retain the confidence of those who do not believe in them, and in order to retain the influence of my example with the children who have been taught to believe such things wrong?

6. Do I take an active and willing part in the movements which make the community better?

7. Do I keep my mind open to new convictions, or do I judge things according to what I have always thought to be right?

8. Do my attitude and example help to strengthen or to weaken the religion of my pupils?

MY INFLUENCE IN THE COMMUNITY.

1. Am I a lifter, or a leaner? Do I push, or ride and drag my feet?

2. What kind of a town would this town be if every person were just like me?

3. Do I send thoughts into the world which do not bless, or cheer, or purify, or heal?

4. Do I ever initiate changes in public opinion, or am I content to wait for someone else to start?

5. What would the community lose if I I should move away?

6. Do I give to the community, or get from it?

7. If I should move away from the community, would I be remembered as a school teacher, or as a fellow citizen and friend?

8. Do I avoid crticism by saying nothing, doing nothing, and being nothing?

MY LEISURE TIME.

1. Is my leisure time spent entirely in the enjoyments of the day, or is a good share of it spent preparing myself for greater efficiency and for a better position?

2. Do I spend my leisure time in good company and wholesome pleasure?

3. Is it probable that I over-estimate the amount of fun I need, and under-estimate the quality of it?

4. Do I take advantage of social hours to make friends? Do I make friends by being one?

5. Is my leisure time wasted time, or is it made profitable in one way or another?

6. Am I a thrifty ant, or a trifling grass-hopper?

MY REALTION TO THE SUPERINTENDENT.

1. Do I try to see things through the superintendent's eyes?

2. Do I boost or criticise?

· 3. Do I go to the superintendent occasionally with words of approval and helpful suggestions, or only with complaints?

4. Do I hand in reports as promptly and as neatly as I expect them from my pupils?

5. Do I try to get ahead by scheming, toadying and currying favor?

6. Can I be intimate and friendly with the superintendent without expecting exceptional favors in my school work?

7. When the superintendent introduces a plan or policy which I am sure will not work, do I take it up half-heartedly in hope that it will fail, or do I get behind it and give it the very best trial possible?

8. Do I insist upon perfect conditions and equipment, or do I, like the Spartan soldier, "add a step to my broken sword"?

9. Do I adjust myself to the superintendent's plans, or expect him to adjust his plans to me?

MY RELATION TO MY ASSOCIATES.

1. Am I really and whole-heartedly loyal to my associates, or do I compromise and nod my head when talking with their enemies?

2. When my words or actions might be misconstrued, do I take the trouble to explain?

3. Do I give my associates credit for being well trained, professional people with a right to their opinions?

. 4. Am I too ready to think my associates have sinister motives?

5. When I have reason for complaint against another teacher, do I take it to that person, or to someone else?

6. Do I ever criticize a fellow teacher to another or to an outsider?

7. Do I realize that my friend's time is valuable and should not be wasted?

8. Is my relation with my associates one
of getting, or of giving?

9. Do I fit easily into the circumstances
confronting me, or do I try to fit them to myself?

10. Am I a square peg in a round hole?

11. Am I a good mixer?

12. Do I stand shoulder to shoulder with
my associates ready to give a strong pull, a
long pull, and a pull all together?

MY RELATION TO THE PARENTS.

1. Am I inclined to hold myself aloof
from the people of the community?

2. Do I make use of programs, societies,
parties, exhibits, etc., to get acquainted with
the parents, and to get them interested in the
school?

3. Do I try to make the school-house and
school equipment of real service in the community?

4. Do I heartily co-operate in the affairs
of the community not connected with the
school?

5. Do I form real friendship among the
parents, or do I cultivate their acquaintance as
a matter of policy?

6. Do I go out of my way to help some
person or to assist in some enterprise?

7. Do I get tied up in too many things
and thus dissipate my energy?

8. Do I clique with the other teachers,
or with some friends in town, or with nobody?

9. If I should leave the community would
I be greatly missed? By whom? Why?

MY SCHOOL ROOM.

1. Is my room well lighted, well ventilated, and clean?

2. Am I willing to be judged by the appearance of my room?

3. Do I enter my room with a feeling of pride, or am I indifferent to it?

4. Have I reached the limit of my ingenuity to make my room attractive with plants, pictures and other decorations, or do I excuse myself with the fact that the school board furnishes no money for that purpose?

5. Have I formed in my pupils the habit of keeping the desk and floor free from paper, pencil-sharpenings, etc.?

6. Is my own desk a good example for the children to follow?

7. Is my room bare or cluttered? Is every space used to the most efficient advantage?

8. Am I ready for visitors all the time?

THE HEALTH OF MY PUPILS.

1. Are my pupils examined physically at least once a year? If not find a local physician who will examine their eyes, nose, throat and teeth at little or no cost.

2. If I teach in a rural school, can I not find means to provide a little medicine cabinet containing some simple remedies, such as witch-hazel, dioxigen, argyrol, absorbent cotton and bandages?

3. Do I talk with my pupils occasionally about colds, contageous diseases, bathing, clothing, deep breathing, care of the teeth, and wholesome food?

4. When the health of a child is being neglected; if he is not bathed, if his lunch is not usually wholesome, or if his teeth need attention, do I talk the matter over tactfully with his parents and try to secure a correction?

5. Do I try to find out the home conditions surrounding each child and look after his health accordingly?

6. Am I able to recognize the symptoms of the more common contageous diseases? Do I look for them every day among my pupils?

7. Is it possible and practicable to furnish each child something hot, such as cocoa or soup, with his lunch, during the winter months?

8. Is my room well ventilated and thoroughly aired as often as necessary?

9. Are my pupils so seated that no child is at a disadvantage relative to sitting posture, sight and hearing?

CHARACTER TRAINING IN MY SCHOOL.

1. Should my pupils get character training from what they learn, or from what they do?

2. Is character building important enough to have a regular period at least once a week?

3. Do I have a regular time every day, or every week, when I have a heart to heart talk with my pupils upon such topics as self-control, politeness, generosity, fair-play, etc., or are the children expected to pick up a good character where they can from the regular school work?

4. Do I expect children to make mistakes in their character training, just the same as in their arithmetic and grammar, and correct these mistakes as carefully, or do I expect them to come to school with well trained characters, and regard violations as personal affronts to me?

5. Do I actively encourage home reading of good books? Have I any plan of keeping good books circulating among the pupils for home reading?

6. Do I look after the children as far as possible outside of school hours, or do I allow my teachings to be counteracted by un-

healthy and immoral influences in the home and on the street?

7. Are my pupils trained to do their best in all of their school activities, or do I accept work as being "good enough?" Has this custom a great influence upon character?

8. Do I deal strictly with a child's tendency to cheat or to deceive?

9. Is personal responsibility required of each child?

10. Do my pupils memorize poems and quotations of a high moral tone? Are they asked to measure their own acts by these standards?

11. Do I habitually weigh the little events of the school day in the moral scale, or am I somewhat careless of the moral significance of these small things in the child's life?

12. Is there a class spirit, class morale and class patriotism in my school?

13. At the close of the term, have I accomplished a degree of character development in each child as noticeable as his development in mental ability?

MY MANAGEMENT.

1. Do I know before going to school in the morning just what I am going to do every minute of the day?

2. Is there a uniformity in the details of my class management which is carefully carried out?

3. Do the pupils rise when reciting?

4. Do they secure recognition by the raised hand before speaking?

5. Is there a regular and orderly way of passing to and from the recitation seats?

6. Is there a uniform way of writing and of handing in written work?

7. Is the black-board work uniform, neat and carefully erased?

8. Do the pupils have regular recitation seats, or do they sit where they wish?

9. Do the pupils stand erect and free from the seat when reciting?

10. Is there a uniform way of holding the text-book when the pupil is reading or explaining a problem?

11. When a pupil cannot answer a question, does he rise and say so, or does he merely remain quiet?

MY GOVERNMENT.

1. Do my pupils look to me as the controlling influence, or are they expected to control themselves?

2. Do I always control myself?

3. Do I make the rules, or do I talk matters over with the pupils and let the rules come as a matter of common desire and consent?

4. In governing, do I realize that each pupil has a personality and a will of his own?

5. Do I sometimes make a rule and forget to enforce it?

6. Do I play and laugh and enjoy things with my pupils?

7. Do my pupils have a share in selecting pictures, etc., for the school room, in managing entertainments, parties, etc.?

8. Do I give my pupils as much respect as I expect from them?

9. Are they respectful in thought and action as well as in word?

10. Do I make self-control in my pupils as much a matter of education as arithmetic and history?

11. Do I appreciate the power of the all-seeing eye?

12. Do I keep saying, "Don't do that," and "You mustn't do that," or do I instantly put the offender to work at something?

13. Is there ever poor order where there is good teaching?

14. Do I ever threaten, and neglect to carry out my threat?

15. When I find myself mistaken, do I acknowledge it fully and frankly at the first opportunity?

MY DISCIPLINE.

1. Do I use corporal punishment for quite a number of offenses, or only as a last resort?

2. Do I depend for success in discipline upon the severity of the punishment or upon the certainty of it?

3. Do I ever punish a child when he does not understand what it is for?

4. Do I ever punish the wrong child, or punish the whole school for the fault of a few?

5. Do I allow my personal likes and dislikes, or my relation to the parents, to enter into my discipline?

6. Do I ever punish a child in anger?

7. Are the methods and severity of my discipline entirely justified on the grounds that the purpose of punishment is to correct the child?

8. Is the offense or the offender the object of my punishment?

9. Do I scold too much?

10. Do I discipline the first case which arises, or do I let the matter run until it gets worse and involves more children?

11. Do I discipline by spells, or all the time?

12. Does my discipline lead directly to the main purpose of making the child self-controlling?

MY ATTITUDE BEFORE THE CLASS.

1. Do I stand or sit during the recitation?

2. Does my presence have a happy or a depressing effect upon the pupils?

3. Am I at ease, or nervous and self-conscious?

4. Is my presence an inspiration to the class?

5. Am I graceful, quiet and orderly in my movements, or is there room for improvement?

6. Is my voice loud or pitched high, or in any way irritating? Has it force and decision?

7. Am I inclined to be too diffident, retiring, weak-voiced, or indecisive?

8. Are my pupils more alert than I am? Do they often evade my sight and hearing?

9. Can I be firm without being unkind?

10. Do I fuss around like an old hen with chickens?

11. Do I assume an air of superiority?

12. Can I be a child with the others and enter into their play and work with real enthusiasm?

MY METHOD.

1. Do I take my cue from the child's needs, ability and interests?

2. What is the most prominent thing in my recitation, the textbook, myself, or the class?

3. Do I talk too much, and thus deprive the pupils of the right of self development?

4. Do I do anything for a child which he can do for himself?

5. Do I lay more emphasis upon the subject I am teaching, or upon cultivating good habits in the children?

6. Do I keep high ideals constantly before the children?

7. Do I use an abundance of oral illustrations, objects, pictures, maps, diagrams, etc., in order to create vivid mental pictures of the thing or situation studied?

8. Do I apply the class work in a practical way to the every day work and needs of the children?

9. Am I acquainted with the peculiar nature of each individual child, or do I know him only as a member of a class?

10. Does my class study a large number of examples, battles, people and facts, or do we select typical individuals and study them thoroughly?

11. Do I use subject matter as an end, or as a tool?

12. Do I teach the children how to study and fix the study habit upon them?

13. Can I get down to the child's level, think as he thinks and talk as he talks?

14. Do I take advantage of play as an educative influence?

15. Do I realize that the pupils can acquire new knowledge only through what they already know, and hence all new knowledge must be related to the old?

16. Do I find out how much the children know about a topic before I begin teaching it?

MY PREPARATION OF THE LESSON.

1. Do I have a regular time for the preparation of tomorrow's work, and make this duty of first importance?

2. Do I make my preparation adequate, or more than adequate?

3. Do I plan each day to do satisfactory work, or to do my best?

4. Do I plan each day to give my class

something new, interesting and of variety, or do I give them some more of the same?

5. After mastering the assigned material in the text-book, do I study "around" my subject in more scholarly works?

6. Do I keep just ahead of the class, or have I a mastery of the whole subject?

7. Do I forego daily preparation "because I have been over the subject before"?

8. Is my daily preparation a burden, or a pleasure?

9. Do I always search the lesson for an opportunity to use objects, pictures or other illustrative material in the recitation?

10. Do I sometimes depend upon inspiration to make up for lack of preparation?

11. Do I always go to a recitation knowing just (1) **What** I am going to do. (2) **Why** I am going to do it, and (3) **How** I am going to do it?

HOW I STUDY.

1. Do I outline the thought of the text on paper as I study it?

2. Does anything short of a complete understanding of the topic satisfy me?

3. Do I make use of (1) reason, (2) hearing, and (3) sight to fix the idea in my mind?

4. Do I stop to think out illustrations and examples as I study?

5. Do I swallow what I read whole or insist upon evidence and proof?

6. Do I study while I study, or merely "spend time on my lesson"?

7. Do I study a subject from the point of view of teaching it?

8. Do I study, crochet, talk and eat peanuts at the same time?

9. Do I take time to think over and digest what I have studied?

MY RECITATION.

1. Do I take a brief time at the beginning of each recitation to prepare the pupil's mind to receive the lesson?

2. Do I arouse the interest and attention of the children in the day's topic by relating it to their lives and interests?

3. Do I give the pupils an aim, or something to look for, at the beginning of each recitation?

4. Do I have a definite aim of my own to accomplish in each recitation?

5. Do I teach each day as if it were my only chance to inspire my pupils?

6. Is most of the recitation time spent giving the pupils new ideas, or in organizing what they know and training them in the efficient use of it?

7. Do I do my work in patches from day to day, or have I a well worked out purpose and outline of the whole subject?

8. When the class goes to sleep should I complain of their listlessness, or stir up the teacher?

9. Do I correct errors in grammar, spelling and pronunciation as they arise?

10. Is every class a writing class, a reading class, a spelling class, a grammar class, and an expression class, or is there a certain time of day when these things are done correctly, and allowed to go as they will the rest of the time?

11. Do I regularly require pupils to make up missed work?

12. How much waste time is there in my recitation?

13. Do I call the roll by name or save that time by noticing what seats are vacant?

14. Do my pupils respond immediately when spoken to?

15. Does work start at the very beginning of the recitation period or are there a number of odds and ends to take some time?

16. Does each recitation have a purpose and go straight to it, or is there a tendency to wander and grope? ·

MY QUESTIONS.

1. Do I ask for a repetition of what is said in the text-book, or for a generalization from those facts?

2. Do my questions persistently apply the lesson to the lives of my pupils?

3. Are my questions thought-provoking?

4. Do my questions call forth the originality of the pupils?

5. Do my questions follow one trunk line of thought and emphasize the important things in it?

5. Do my questions arouse interest and enthusiasm?

7. Do I call upon a pupil before asking a question, or do I ask my question, and, after the whole class have thought, call upon some one to answer?

8. Do my questions cling close to the topic under discussion and hold the thought of the class to that topic?

9. Do I know the next best question at any stage of the recitation?

10. Do I tell an answer before the pupil's resourses have been exhausted?

11. Have I fallen into the habit of repeating answers, or of saying, "That's right," "All right," or "That's wrong," after each answer?

12. Do my questions train the child to think, or to guess?

MY NOTE-BOOKS.

1.   Are the note-books kept for my benefit, or for the benefit of the pupils?

2.   Do I realize that keeping a note-book carefully, or slovenly, has an important moral influence upon the child?

3.   Do I make definite just what material is to be kept in the note-book?

4.   Do I require uniformity in the kind of note-book, whether it be kept in ink or pencil, etc?

5.   Do the note-books contain pictures and other attractive material collected by the children, or just their required notes?

6.   Do the children take pride in their note-books?

7.   Do I realize the importance of a good note-book as an incentive to good work and as an aid in drill and in review?

8.   Is the knowledge in the note-book in the child's head, or merely in the note-book?

9.   Are the note-books kept up to date and thus reinforce the recitation, or are they allowed to get behind until the material is stale and half forgotten?

10.   Is the note-book a pretty good index of the quality and quantity of work done by the pupils?

11.   Do I often find a good student with a poor note-book or a poor student with a good one?

MY ILLUSTRATIVE MATERIAL.

1.   Am I in the habit of collecting and mounting pictures and post cards which are useful as illustrative material in history, geography, literature, agriculture and nature study?

2. Have I secured from various manufacturers of flour, clothing, dress-goods, shoes, food-stuffs, farm machinery, etc., samples showing the development of those industries and the steps in the process of manufacture? Do I appreciate the value of this material in teaching the industrial side of geography and history?

3. Is it profitable work for the children to make collections of their own and assist in a collection for the school?

4. Do I collect and file away for reference the bulletins and and pamphlets pertaining to my work issued by the Bureau of Education, by the state university, by the state department of education and by the various learned societies of the United States?

5. Do I clip freely from newspapers and magazines and file these clippings for use in my classes?

6. Do I take, and read, a professional magazine dealing with my work?

7. Is everything I see and hear "grist for my mill"?

MY USE OF THE TEXT-BOOK.

1. Am I inclined to be a slave to the text-book and to make my pupils so?

2. Do my pupils consider their preparation of the lesson complete when they have learned what is said in the text-book, or do they regard those facts only as the material with which to construct their opinions and understanding of the whole subject, just as lumber, stone and plaster are not a house, but merely the material to be used in its construction?

3. Do I eliminate from the text those things which are not applicable and useful in

the community and to my children, and add useful things not given, or do I teach the text as it is without much thought of its usefulness?

4. Do I have the text-book open before me during the recitation? Is this fair to the children?

5. Do I regard the text-book as sufficient authority, or do I appeal to reason and to other sources?

MY ASSIGNMENTS.

1. Am I careful in my assignments and state very definitely just what is to be done, and **how?**

2. Are my assignments made orally, **or** written on the black-board so that a misunderstanding is impossible?

3. Is a misunderstanding of the assignment ever allowed to pass as an excuse for not having a lesson?

4. Do I outline the next lesson, showing the main things to be noted, or is the pupil's first introduction to each lesson obtained from him study of the text-book?

5. Is my assignment of the next lesson made carefully at the beginning of the recitation or, hurriedly at the close of it?

6. Do my assignments to supplementary reading state the book, the chapter, and pages, or is a topic given leaving pupils to find it where they can?

7. Is the assignment of the next lesson made by topic, or by pages?

8. Do I prepare the advance lesson **before** it is assigned?

9. Do I assign merely the amount to be studied for the next lesson, or do I show the pupils how to study it?

MY STUDY PERIODS.

1. Do I have study periods when the whole room can study without interruption or annoyance?

2. Are my pupils busy? Are they merely occupied, or are they working to a purpose?

3. Do I notify the parents what lessons their children are expected to study at home, and ask their co-operation in securing regular and careful home study?

4. Am I cultivating in the pupils habits of regular and careful study?

5. Do I use the study period to teach the pupils how to study?

6. Do I have a supply of extra work, profitable to the student and to the school, which I can ask the brighter pupils to do during study period, after they have prepared their lessons?

7. Do I permit lip study, frequent speaking, frequent leaving the room, or any disturbing influence, during the study periods?

MY REVIEWS.

1. Do I review at the end of a certain number of weeks, or at the end of a topic?

2. Do I review in the same way I taught the subject the first time over, or do I make the review a new view?

3. Am I careful to make my review a repetition of the thought process, not merely a repetition by the lips or hands?

4. Do I review so many lesser facts that the main points are not made to stand out clearly?

5. Do I have a short review at the close of every topic, in such a way that the material is organized in the child's mind under the topical heading?

6. Do my reviews make the child see the relation between each topic and the whole subject?

MY TESTS AND EXAMINATIONS.

1. Why do I give an examination?

2. Do I give an examination for any other reason than to comply with requirements?

3. Do I place too much emphasis upon the examinations as a final means of grading pupils?

4. Do I make the examination an educative thing in itself?

5. Do I examine any mental faculty except the memory? .

6. Do my questions emphasize the reasoning power?

7. Do I examine the child's ability to use what he knows?

8. Do my questions place any premium upon originality?

9. In marking the papers, do I consider such matters as the child's nervousness, his health at the time, fatigue, etc.?

10. Is every examination a test in English, in spelling, in penmanship and in neatness, and marked accordingly?

MY LIBRARY.

1. Do I fail to find time to read, or do I read a great deal and fail to find time for some other things?

2. If I should take the text-books from my library, would a stranger recognize my profession from looking at the remaining books?

3. Do I add some new and good books to my library each year?

4. Do I measure the value of my library by the number of good books I have, or by the use obtained from them by myself and my friends?

5. Have I tried giving an entertainment to buy books for the school?

6. Do I secure interest in the school library by giving the children a share in selecting new books?

7. In making up my library and the school library, have I taken advantage of the vast mine of free material to be obtained on all subjects from the government, from the state, from the state university and from various learned societies and reform organizations of the United States?

8. Are the books in the school library selected mainly because of the values of the subject matter, or for the purpose of making the children like books and enjoy reading them?

9. Do I make a special effort to secure home reading of good books by the pupils?

10. Do I have a plan of keeping good books from the school library, or from my own library, circulating among the pupils?

11. Would more home reading of good books tend to prevent or lessen the harmful reading often done by pupils?

12. Would more home reading improve the pupil's English?

MY RESULTS.

1. Have I educated the whole child, or just his mind?

2. Have I given too much emphasis to what the child knows, and not enough to what he is and what he can do?

3. Assuming that education should develop and train the child physically, mentally and morally, have I neglected any one or two of these phases?

4. Have I actually imbued the child with high ideals until they are a part of him, or has he merely been exposed to them?

5. Do my teachings function in the lives of the children?

6. Have I formed in the children definite habits of honesty, truthfulness, loyalty, helpfulness, generosity, kindness, industry, perseverance, efficiency, and regard for others?

7. Have I trained the children to do things for themselves?

8. Have I improved the children physically, and relieved them of any physical handicaps which troubled them?

9. Have my pupils acquired habits of cleanliness, of sensible diet, and of sane living?

10. Have my pupils acquired a liking for the things they have studied, a desire to know more about them and to use them?

11. Do my pupils leave my instruction with a sincere desire to do a man's work, or a woman's work, in the world?

12. Are my pupils better and stronger morally because of my influence?

13. Do my pupils show good training in their habits and manners?

CPSIA information can be obtained
at www.ICGtesting.com
Printed in the USA
BVHW041056271218
536518BV00006B/149/P